Simeon's Secret

LUKE 2:22-35 FOR CHILDREN

Written by Janice Kramer

Illustrated by Betty Wind

Concordia Publishing House

ARCH Books
© 1969 CONCORDIA PUBLISHING HOUSE, ST. LOUIS, MISSOURI
CONCORDIA PUBLISHING HOUSE LTD., LONDON, E. C. 1
MANUFACTURED IN THE UNITED STATES OF AMERICA

A happy man was Simeon.
This is the reason why:
The Lord had told him long ago
that he would never die
until he saw the Promised One,
the Great Messiah, God's own Son.
Old Simeon believed. He knew
that God would make His word come true.

He kept his secret years and years
and waited every day.
But Simeon was not a man
to waste his time away.
Each morning he'd get out of bed
and comb the hair upon his head
and hurry to the temple, where

he'd worship God with praise
and prayer.

Then afterward, as he would stroll
along the winding street,
the children of Jerusalem
would follow at his feet.

They'd say to him, "Please stop awhile!"
Then he would look at them and smile
and sit right down upon the ground
with all the children gathered round.

And then he'd tell a story;
what a story it would be!
Perhaps the one about the funny
little dancing flea

or one about the sneezing snail

or Wumple-Doo, the wheezing whale.

The boys and girls missed not a word;
such stories they had never heard!

The little ones loved Simeon.
He was the children's friend.
But still he longed to see the Child
that God Himself would send.
Would He be dark? Would He be fair?
Would He have straight or curly hair?
And would that Child of holy birth
feel loved and wanted here on earth?

One morning early Simeon
was wakened from his bed
by people talking on the street.
He heard what one man said:
"In Bethlehem I heard the word
that Christ is born, the promised Lord.
There in a stable, shepherds say,
they saw Him on a bed of hay."

"Can this be true?" cried Simeon.
"Lord, show the Child to me."
He prayed and waited day by day
the newborn Christ to see.

"Arise, good Simeon, arise
and go without delay,
for in the temple you will find
Him now — this very day!"

It was the voice of God he heard,
and Simeon obeyed His word.
He hurried down the winding street
as fast as he could move his feet.

He climbed the
temple stairway with
a quick and easy stride
and stood right by
the door to watch
as people went inside.

His eyes looked into every face
that passed him in that holy place.
And then he saw, amid the crowd,
a sight that made him cry aloud:

A mother and a father
with a little baby boy!
Old Simeon could not hold back
his happiness and joy.

He hurried over to the Child,
and Jesus looked at him and smiled.

Good Simeon could hardly speak,
for tears were running down his cheek.

He took the Baby in his arms
and held Him to his chest.
"O God of mercy, God of might,
Thy name be ever blest!
I've seen Thy Son, the Promised One.
Now let Thy holy will be done,
and take me soon to live with Thee
in heaven for eternity."

With that he turned and started home
along the winding street.
And there, of course, the children came
to trail behind his feet.
"O Simeon, please stop awhile!"
He answered with a friendly smile
and sat right down upon the ground
with all the children gathered round.

He didn't tell the story
of the flea or of the snail.
He didn't even tell the one
about the funny whale.

The story that he told to them
was of the Babe of Bethlehem!
And all the children, big and small,
enjoyed that story best of all.

DEAR PARENTS:

Luke tells us about Simeon's secret: "It had been revealed to him by the Holy Spirit that he should not see death before he had seen the Lord's Christ" (Luke 2:26). Simeon believed this special message from the Lord. He served the Lord and praised Him in the temple. He waited in hope for the day when he would see the promised Messiah.

Our story describes Simeon as a warm, friendly man who loved to tell stories to children. He must have been a loving, fatherly person because he was in touch with God. We hope your child will sense this quality in Simeon.

But most of all, we hope you will help your child feel Simeon's joy as he holds the promised Child Jesus in his arms. Years and years of waiting, believing, and hoping are fulfilled. Now Simeon is ready to depart in peace. The Lord has kept His secret promise, and Simeon has seen the salvation God prepared for all people.

The Child Simeon held in his arms is the salvation God has prepared for you and for your child. He is the Son of God, who became a human person to live, die, and rise again.

Simeon's secret is no longer a secret but good news for the world. You can help your child share the Good News of Jesus Christ today.

THE EDITOR